The Open-String Book
for Violin

by Cassia Harvey

CHP249

©2014 by C. Harvey Publications All Rights Reserved.

www.charveypublications.com - print books
www.learnstrings.com - PDF downloadable books
www.harveystringarrangements.com - chamber music

The Open String Book for Violin

1. Open E String

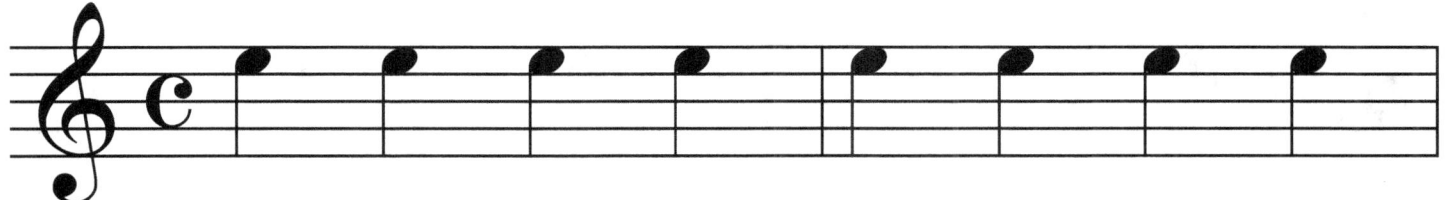

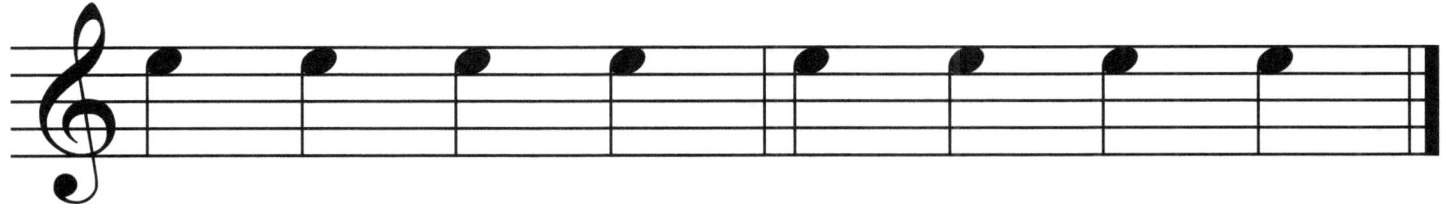

2. Open E with Rests

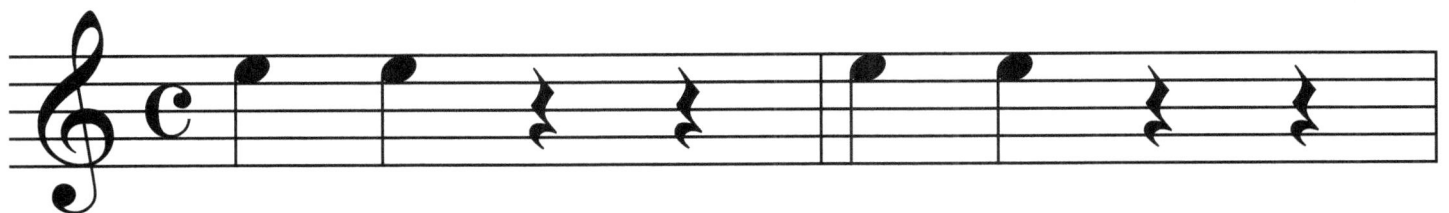

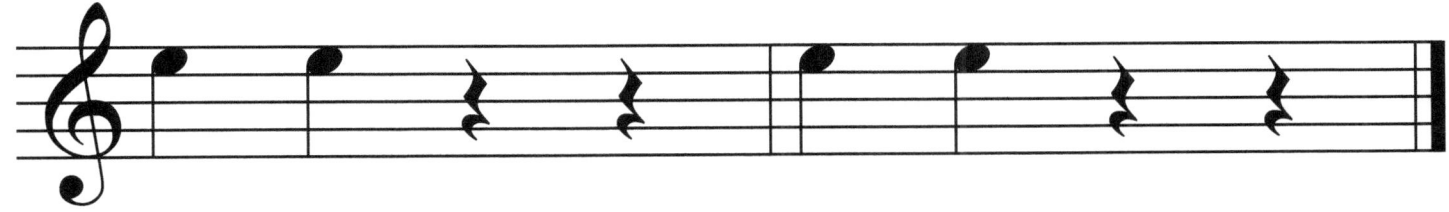

©2014 C. Harvey Publications All Rights Reserved.

3. Open E with More Rests

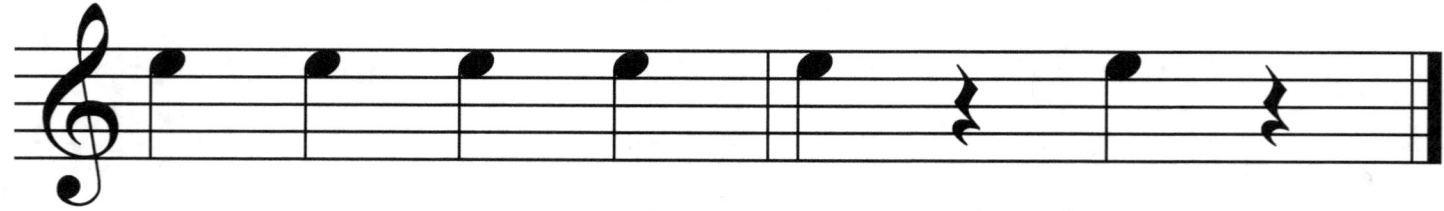

4. Open A String

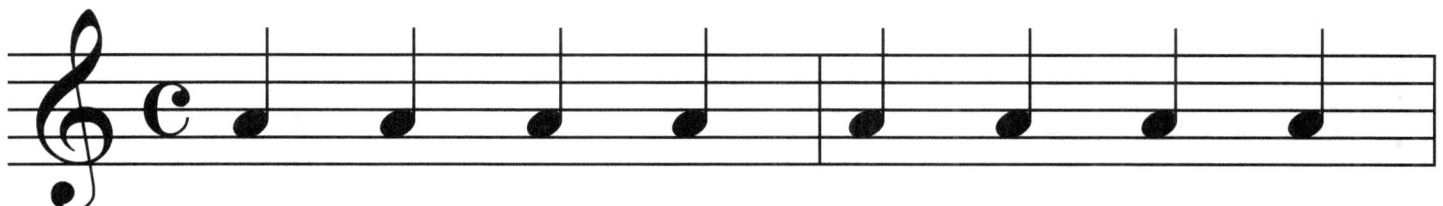

5. Open A with Long-Short-Short

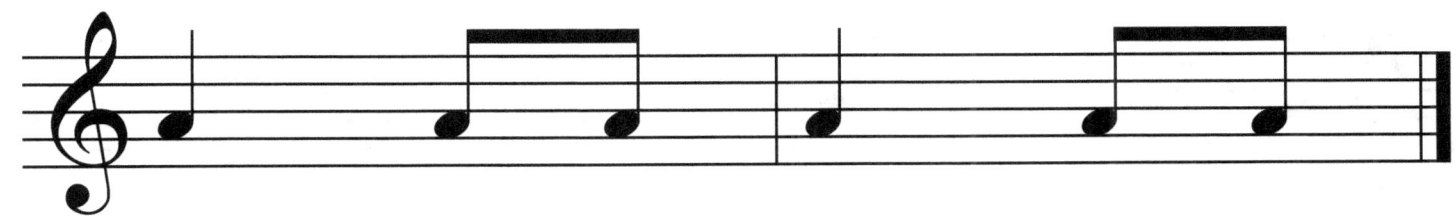

©2014 C. Harvey Publications All Rights Reserved.

6. Open A with Rests

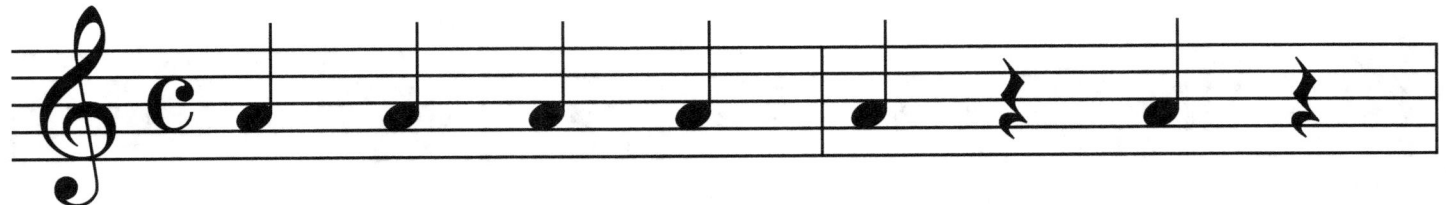

7. Open A with Half Notes

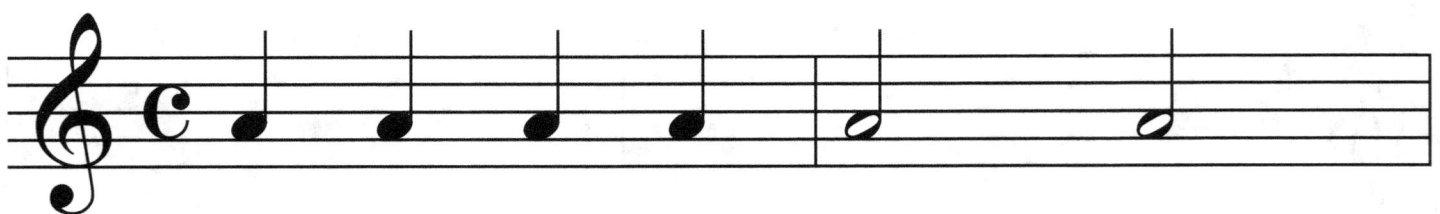

8. Open E and A

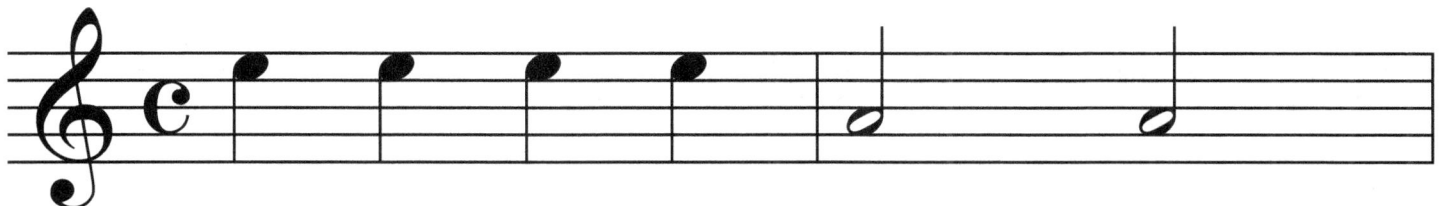

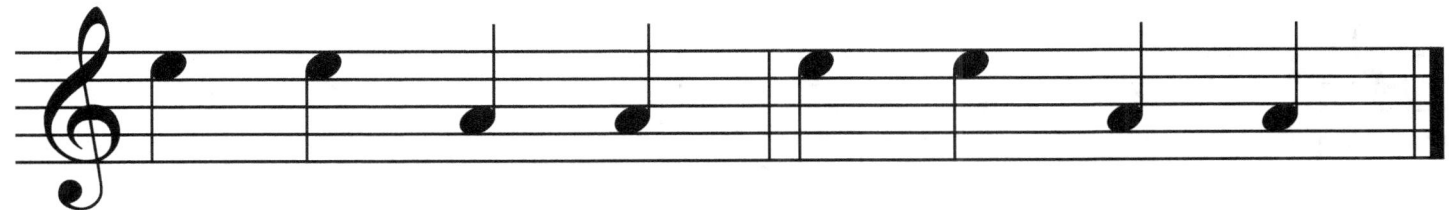

9. Open E and A Double Stops

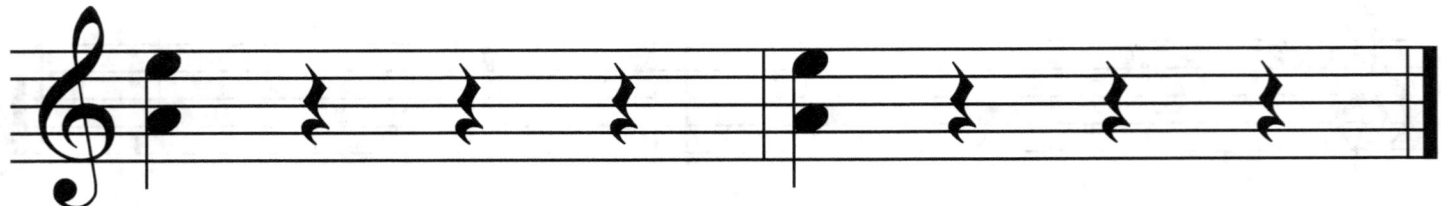

10. Open D String

11. Open D with Short-Short-Long

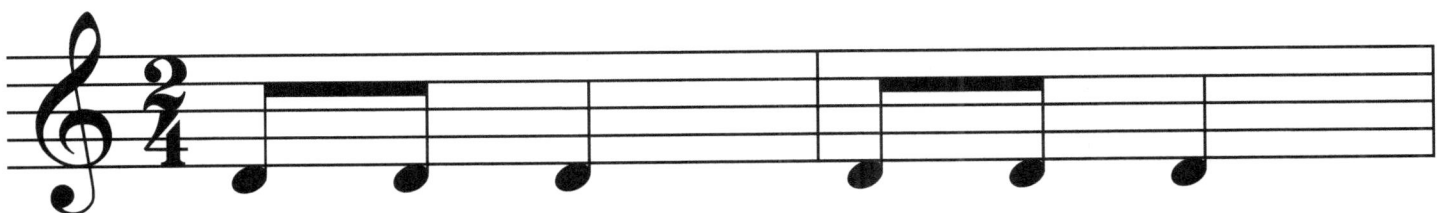

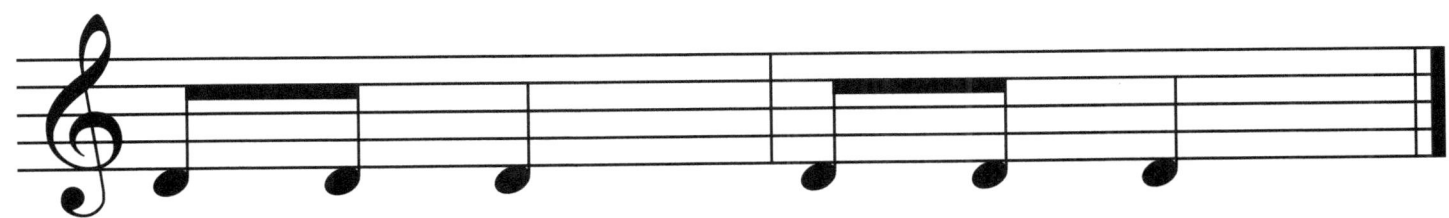

12. Open D with Rests

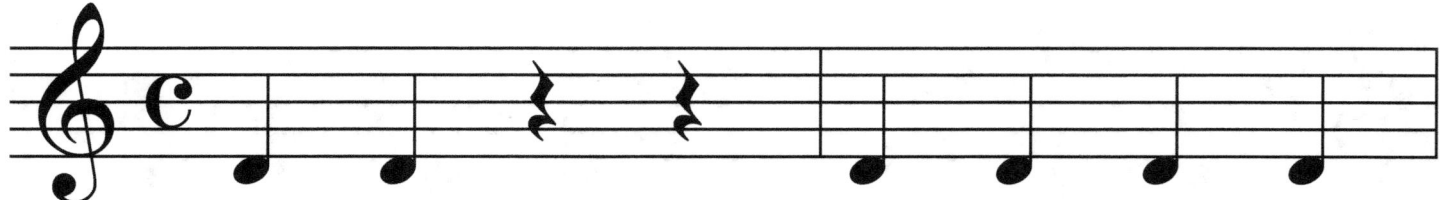

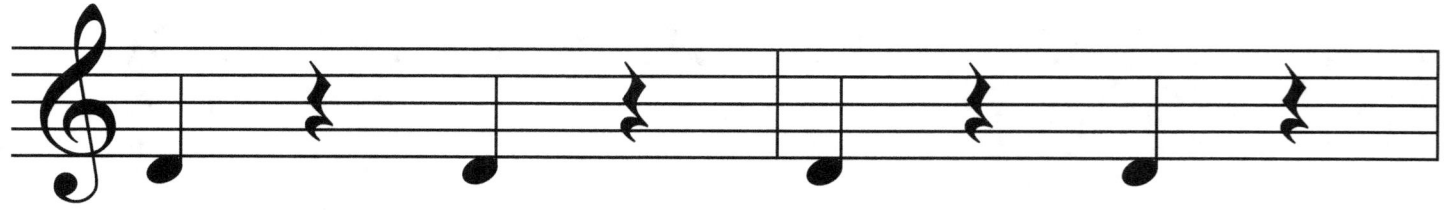
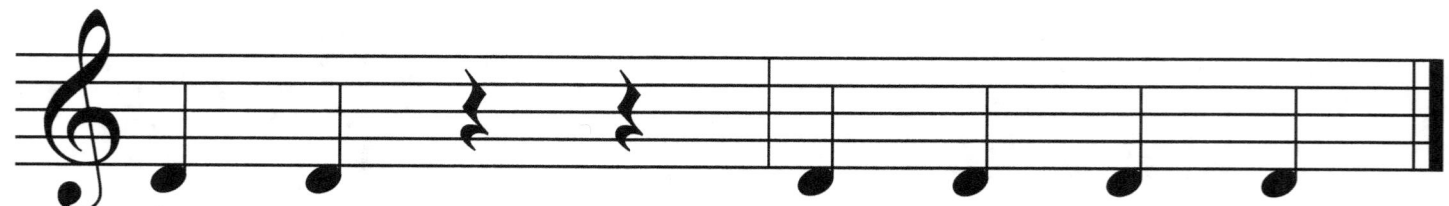

13. Open D and A

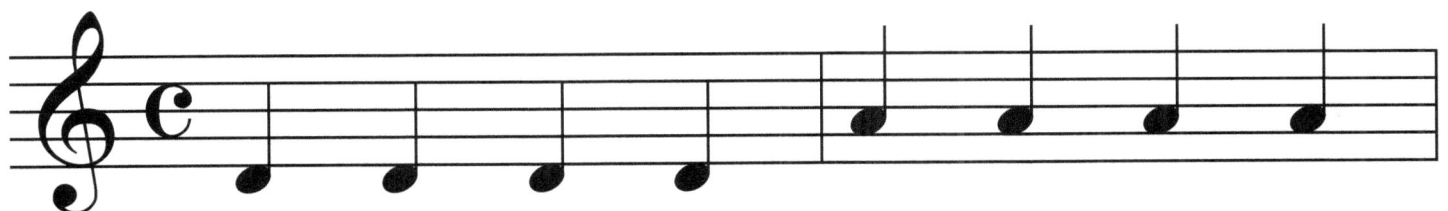

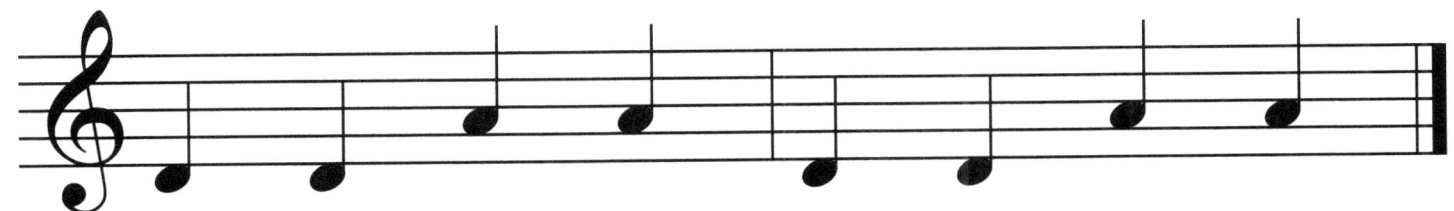

14. Open G

15. Open G with Rests

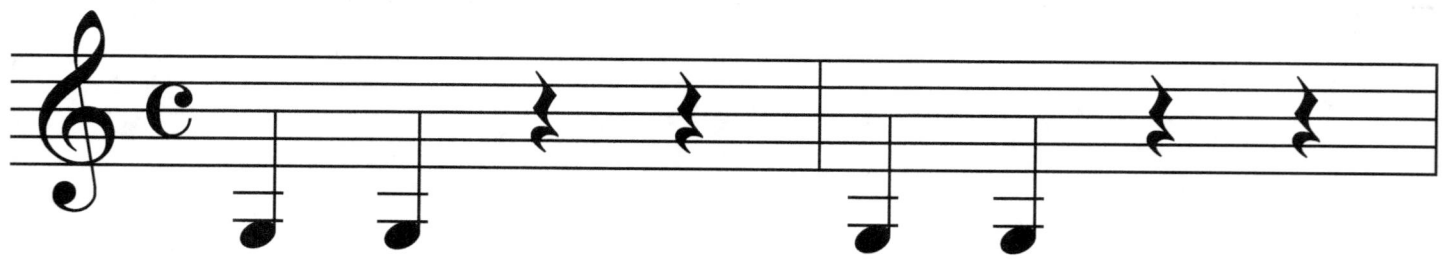

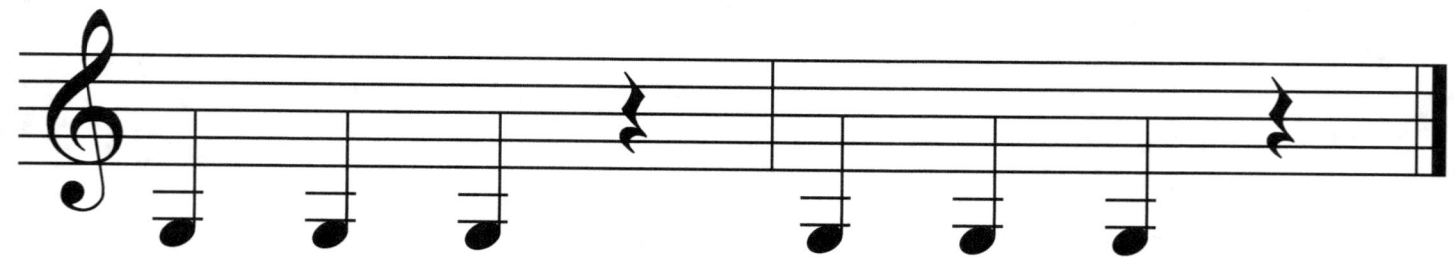

16. Open G with Short-Short-Long

17. Open G and D

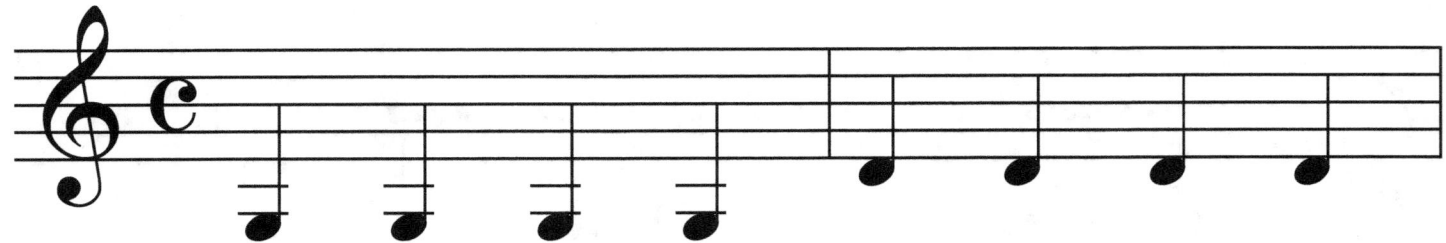
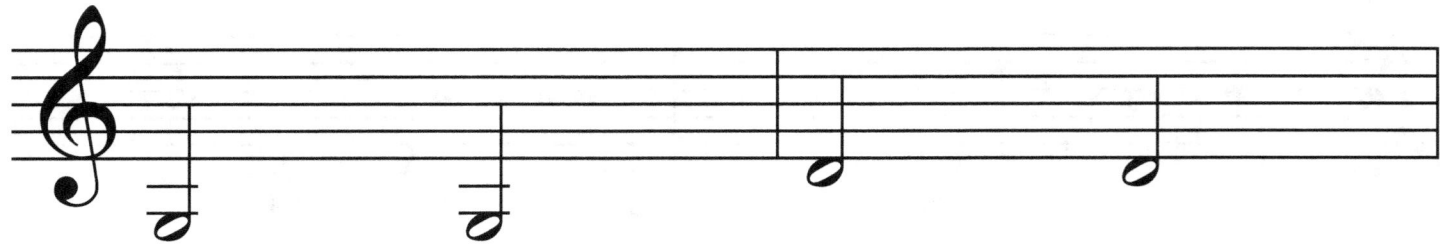
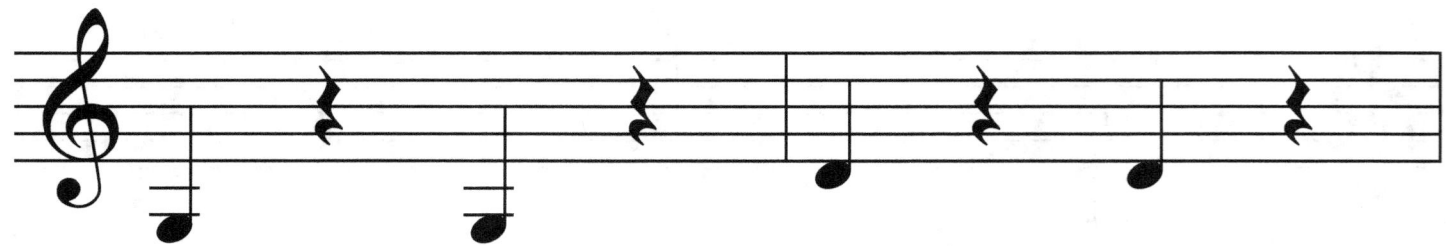
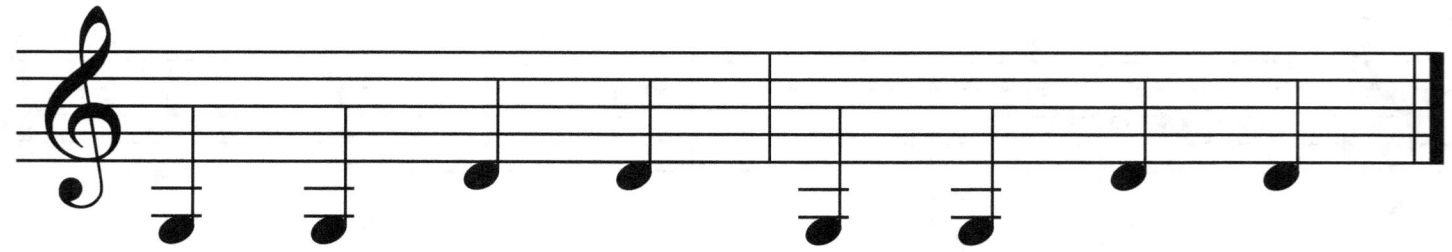

18. Double Stops on E and A

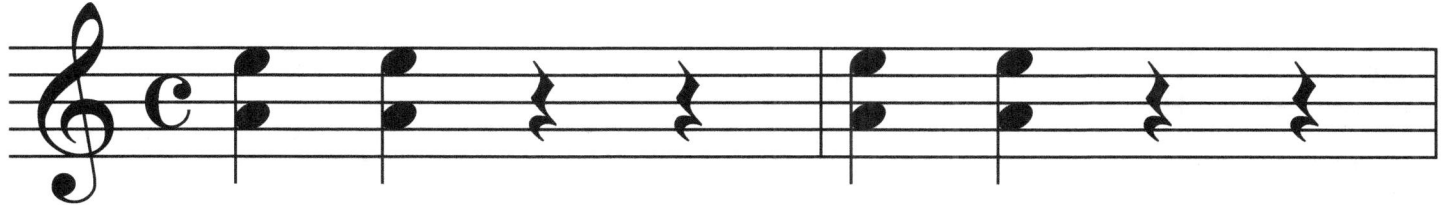

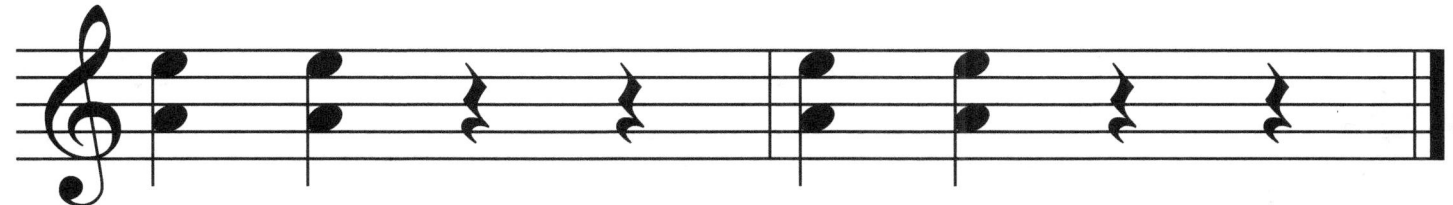

19. Double Stops on A and D

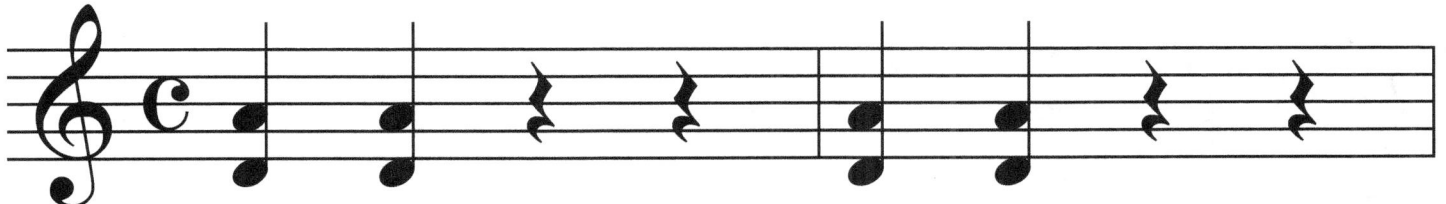

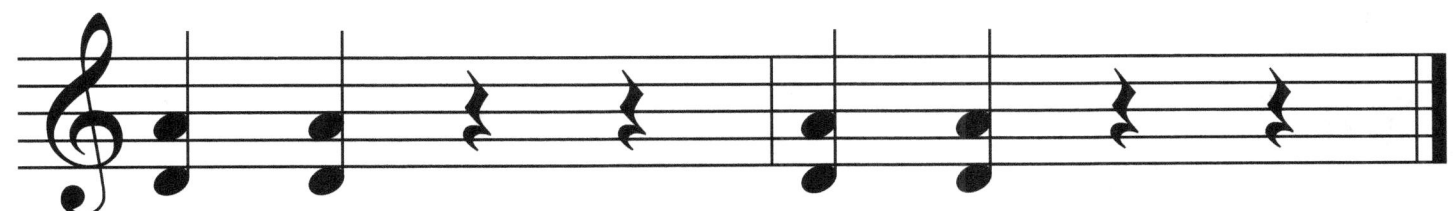

20. Double Stops on D and G

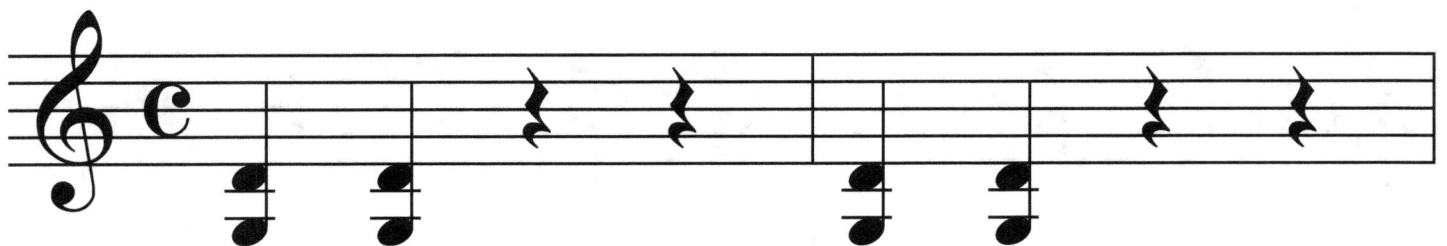

21. Marching in Double Stops

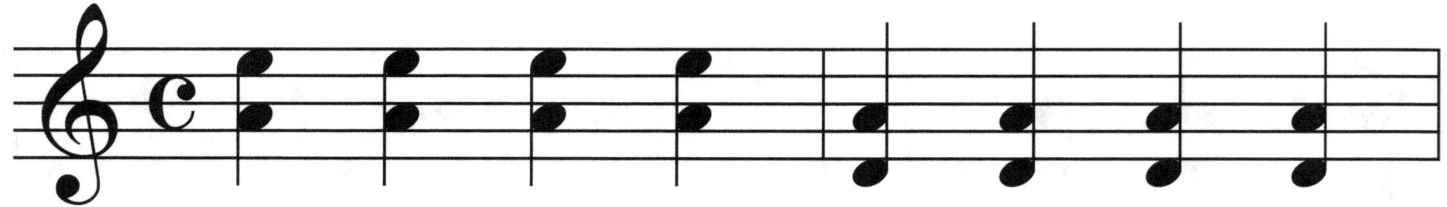

22. Counting to 3

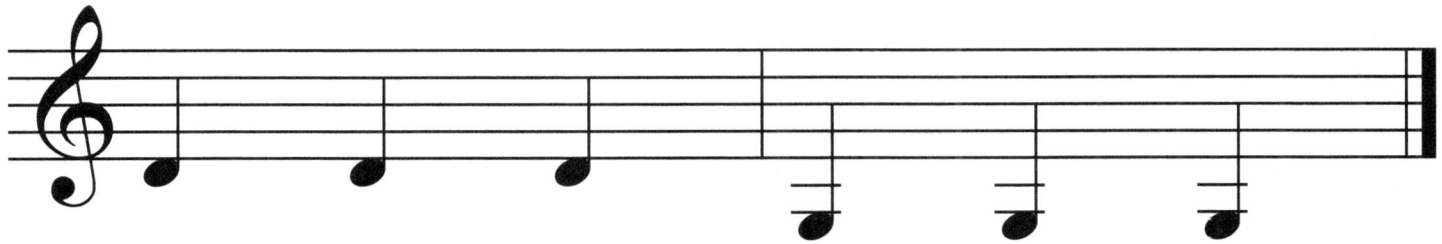

23. Three Beats in a Measure

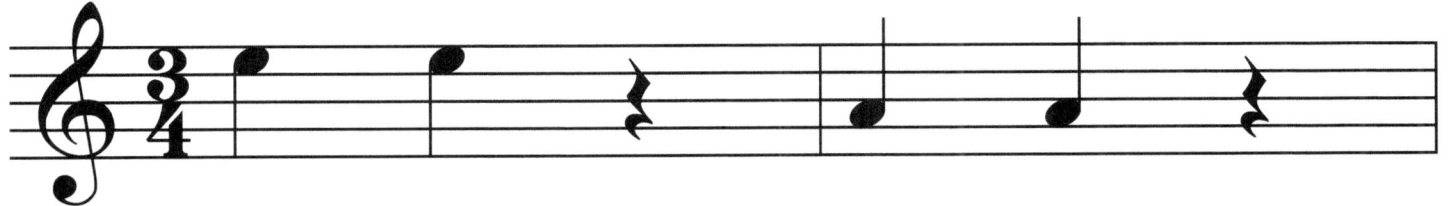

24. Three Beats on D

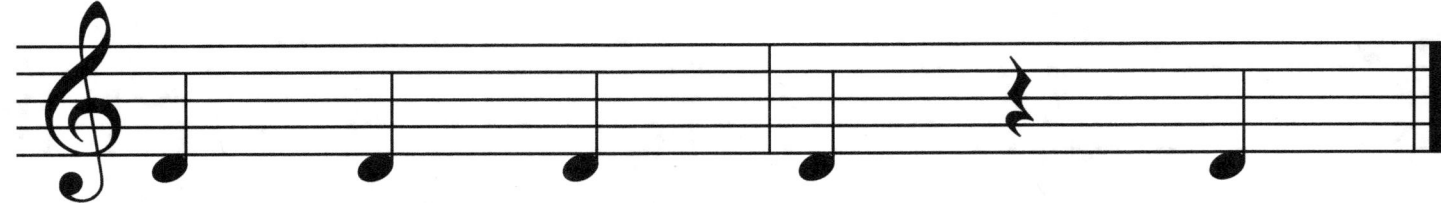

25. Three Beats on G

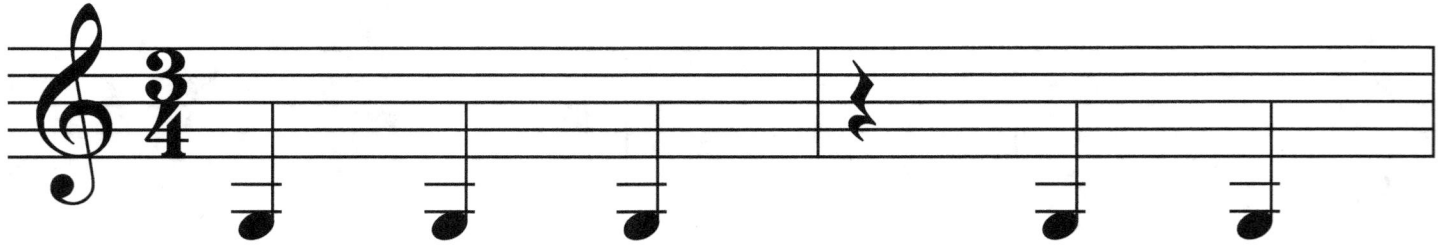

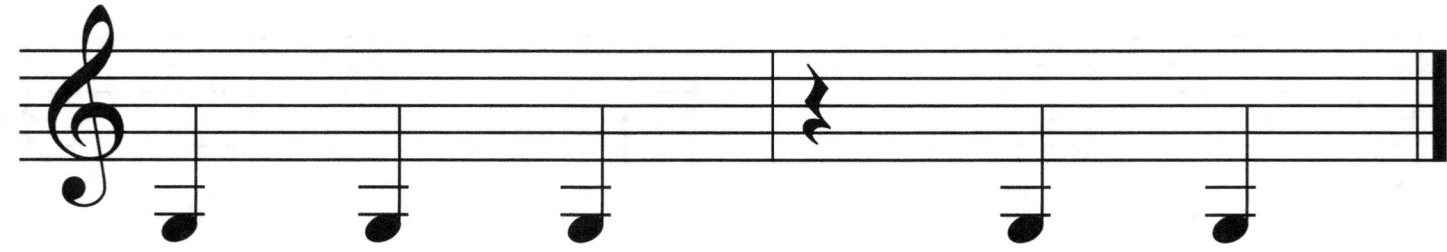

26. Three Beats in a Measure

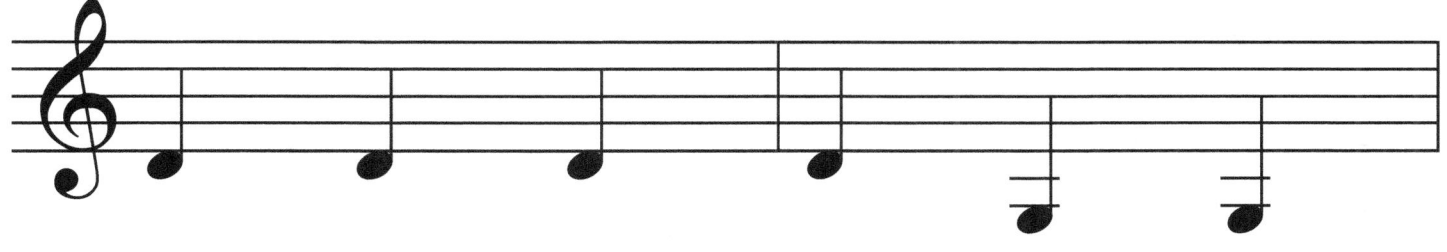
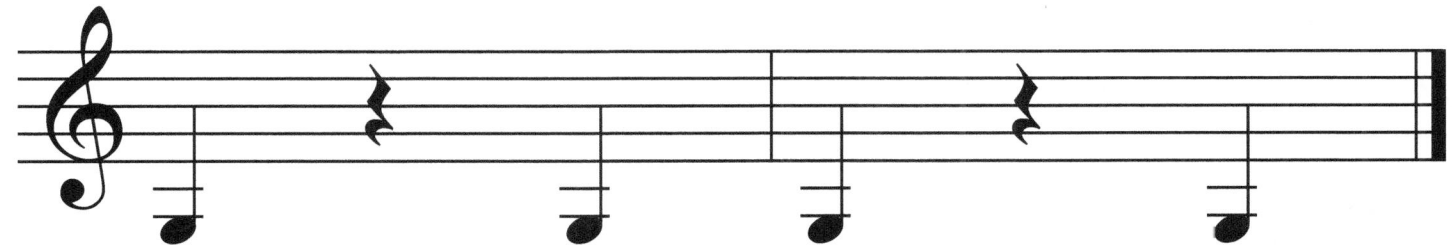

27. Two in a Bow on E and A

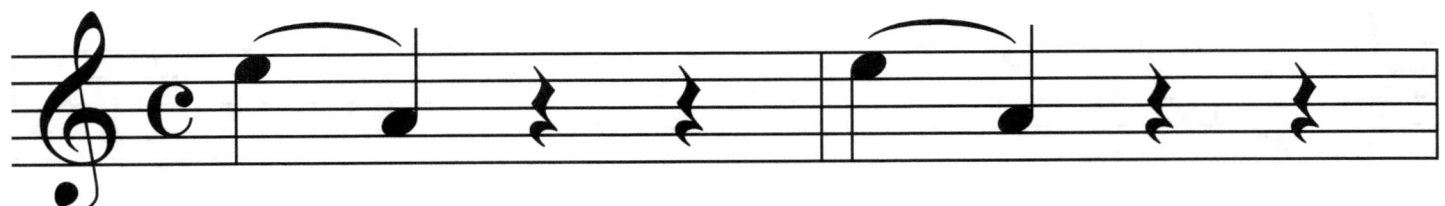

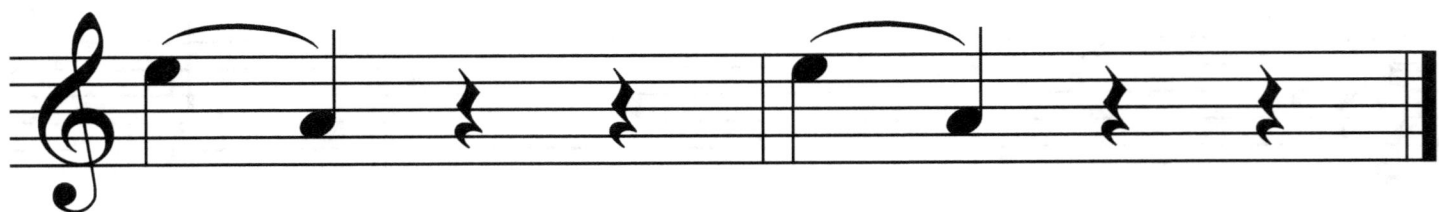

28. Two in a Bow on A and D

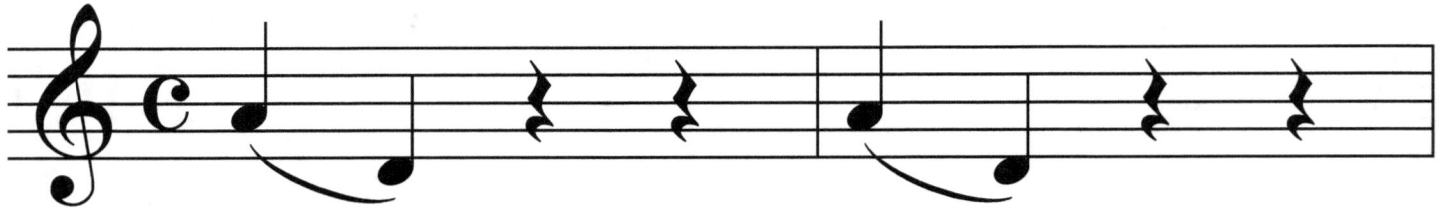

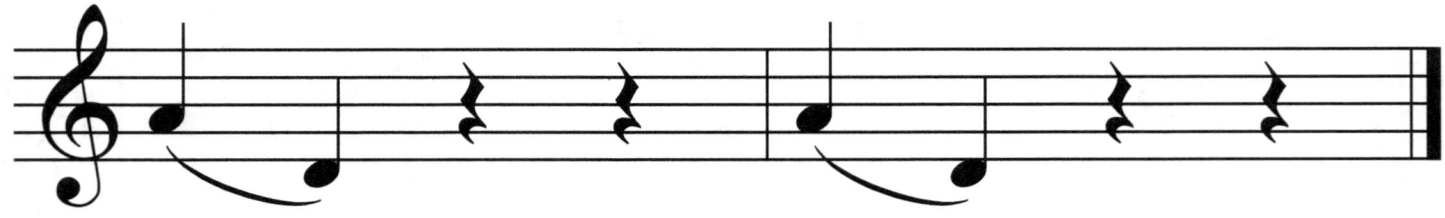

29. Two in a Bow on D and G

30. Two in a Bow on A and E

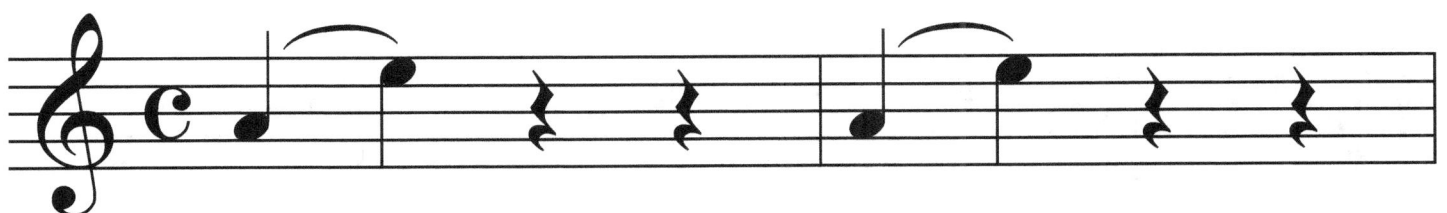

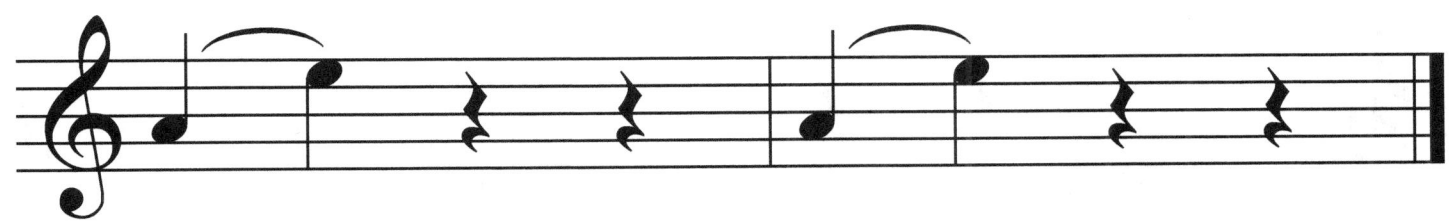

31. Two in a Bow on D and A

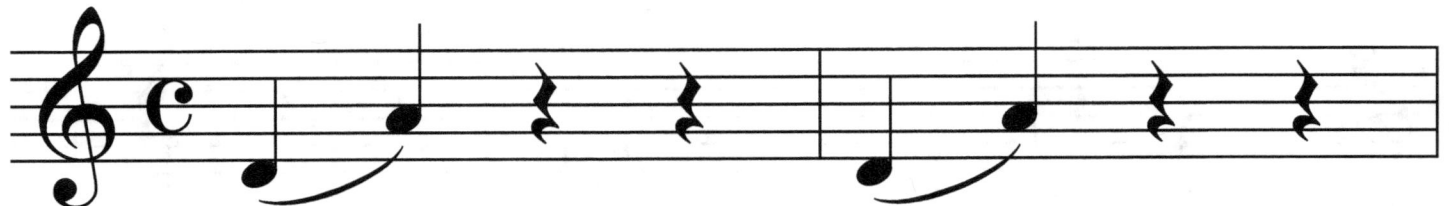

32. Two in a Bow on G and D

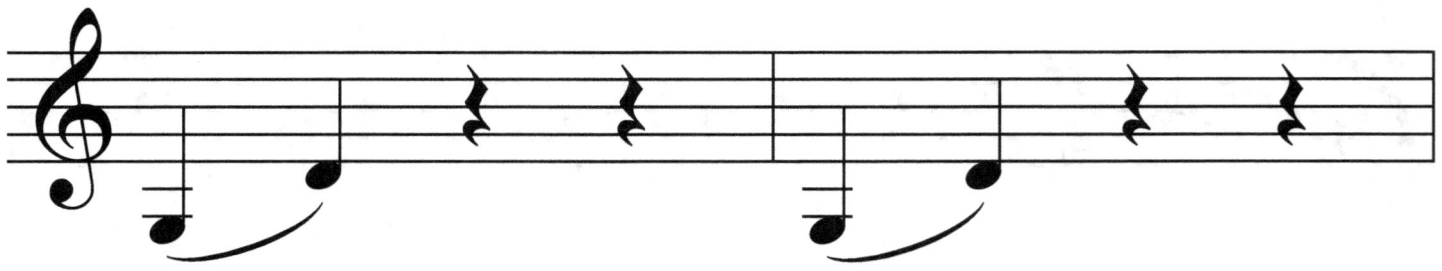
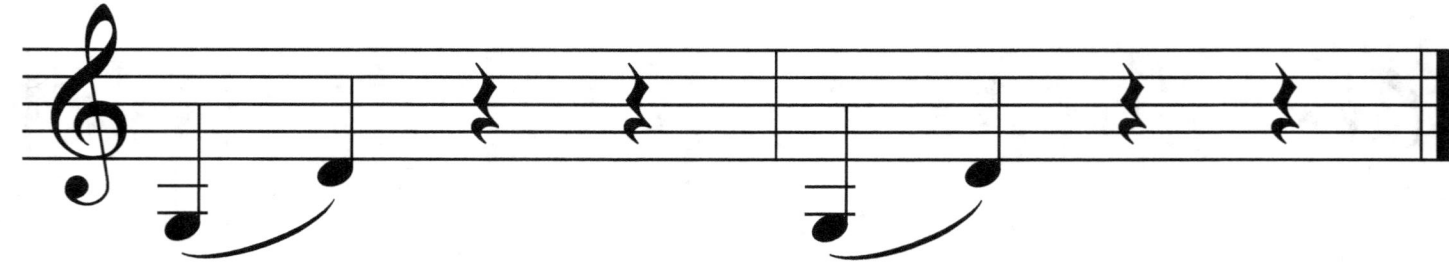

33. Two in a Bow without Rests

34. Two in a Bow on D and A

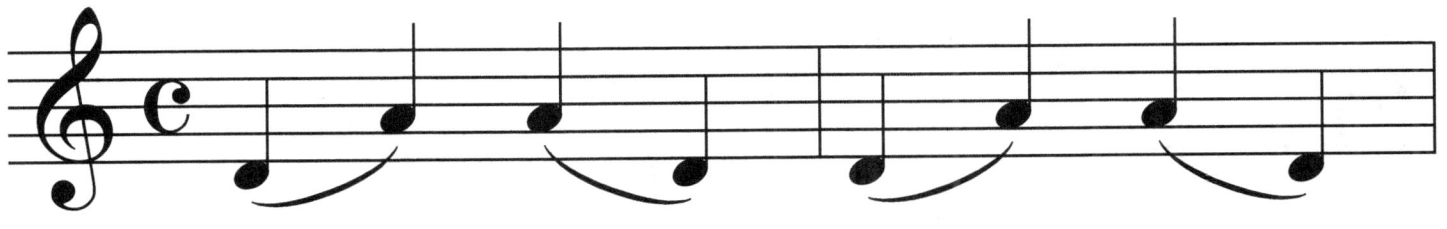

35. Two in a Bow on G and D

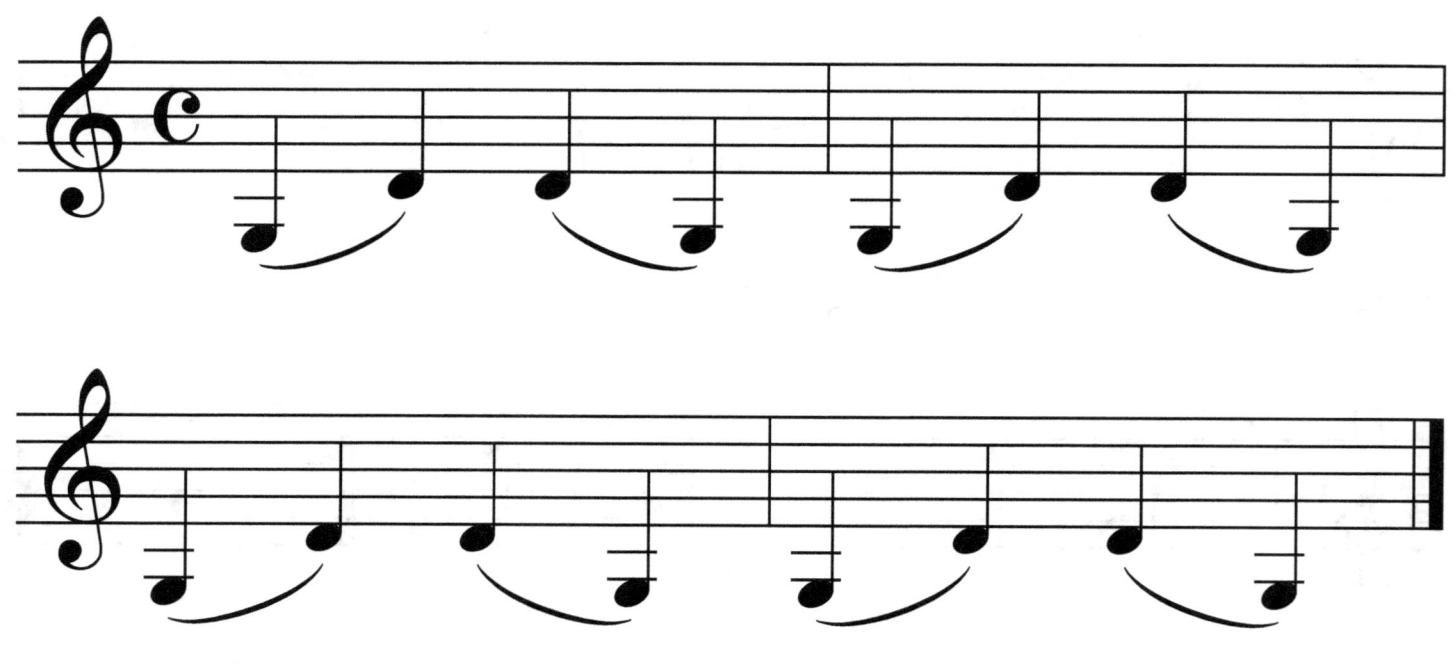

36. Slow and Fast Bows on D and G

37. Slow and Fast Bows on A and D

38. Slow and Fast Bows on A and E

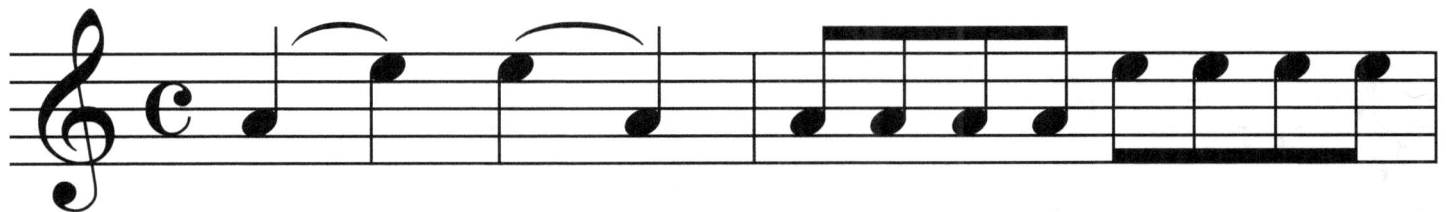

39. Two in a Bow Exercise

40. Whole Notes

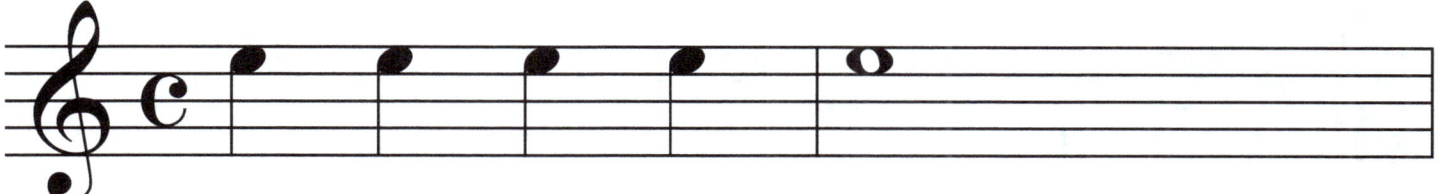

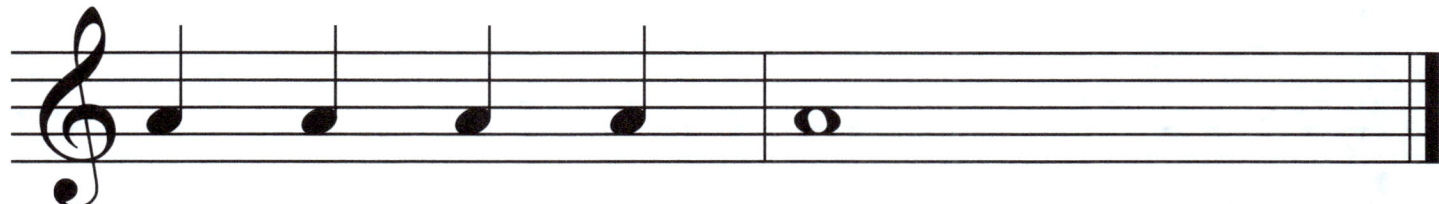

41. Half Notes and Whole Notes

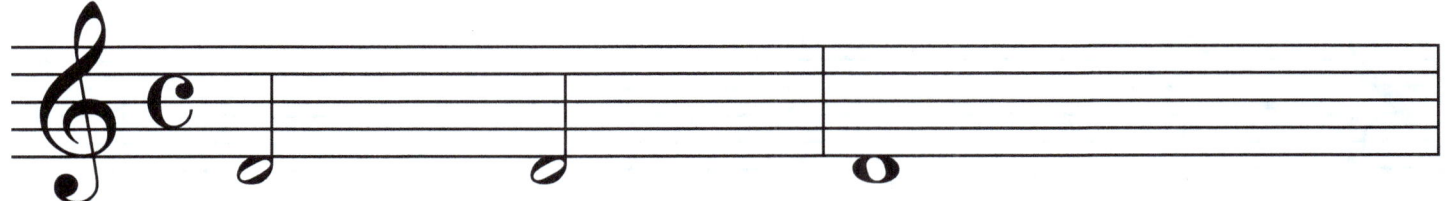

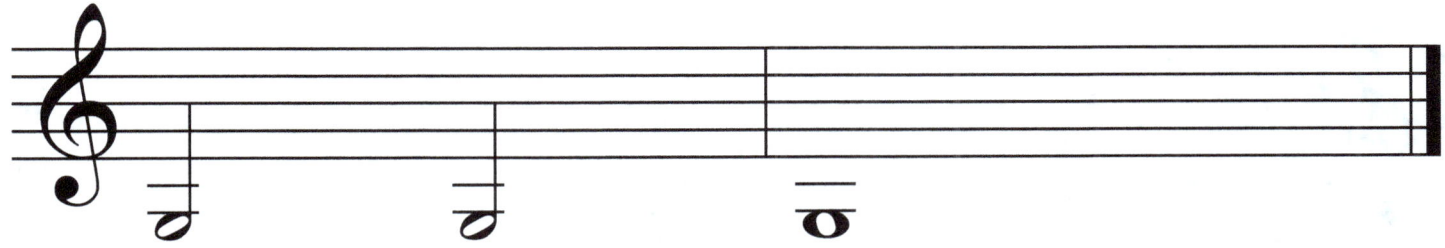

42. Counting to 1, 2, and 4

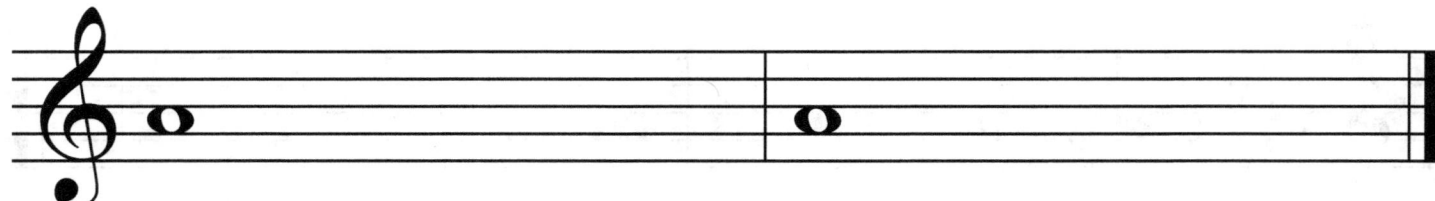

43. Counting to 1, 2, and 4

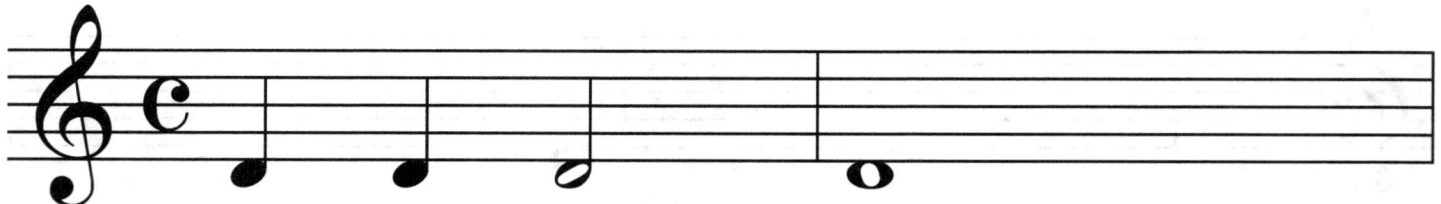

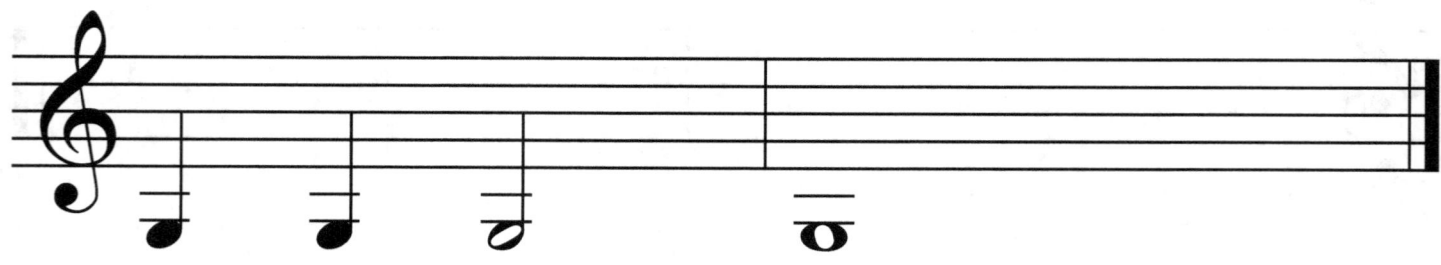

44. Counting to 1, 2, and 4

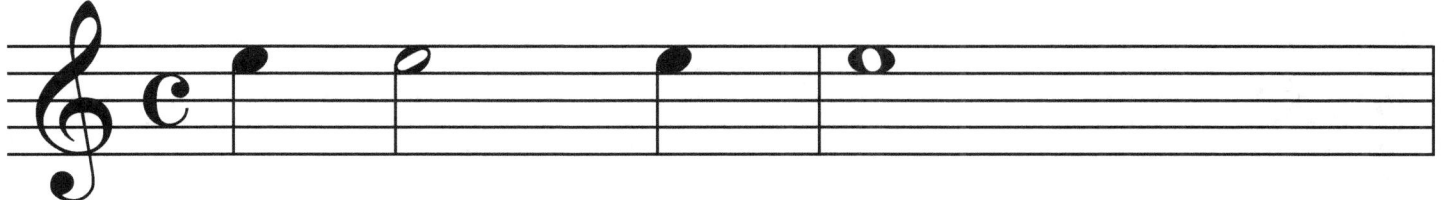

45. Counting to 1, 2, and 4

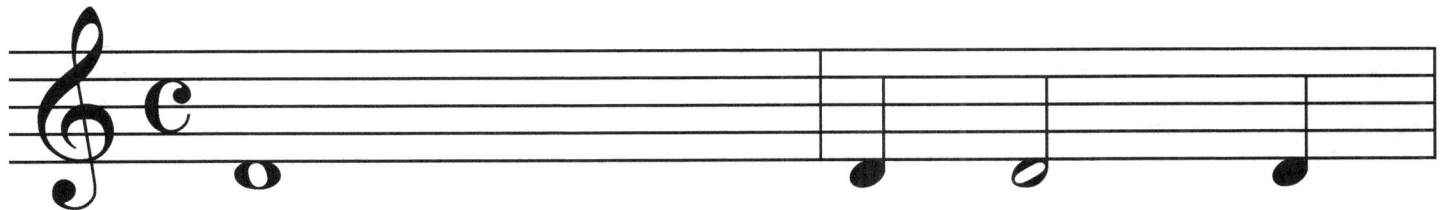

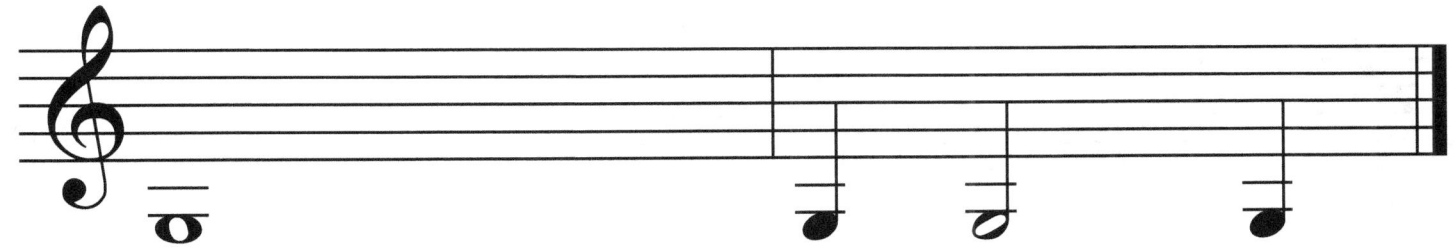

46. Counting and String Crossing

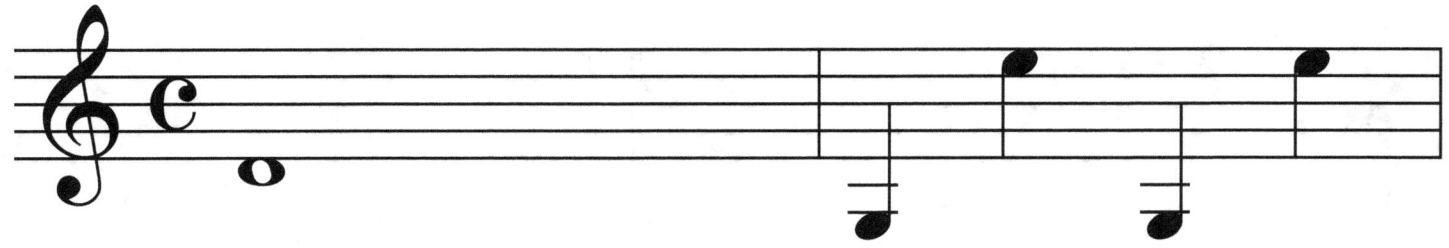

47. More Counting and String Crossing

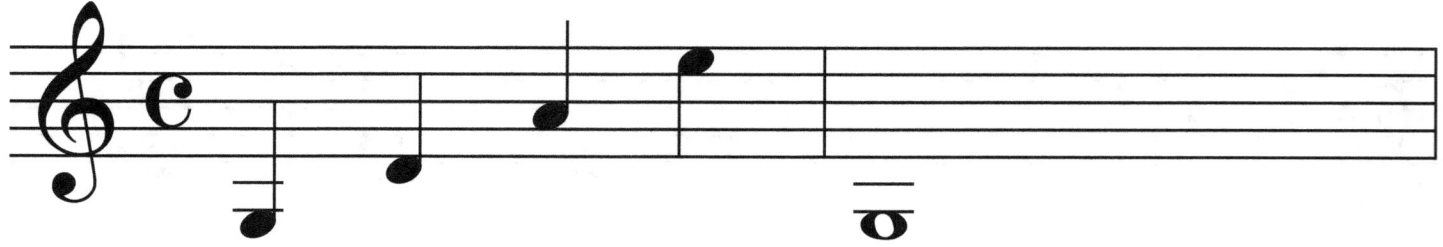

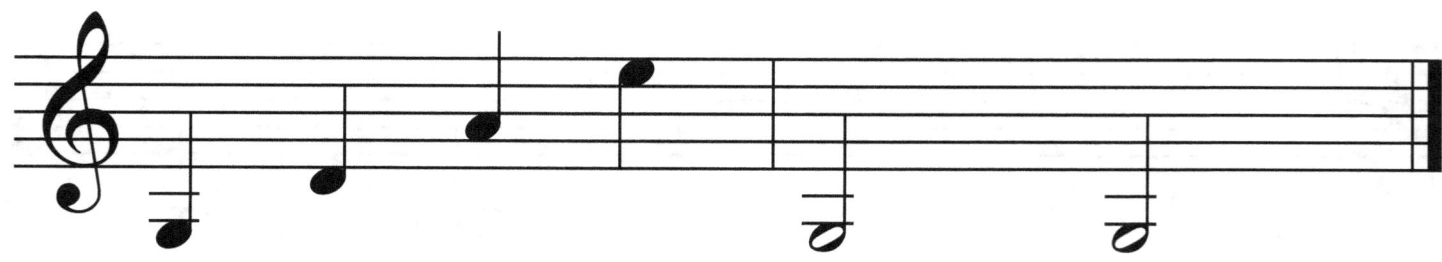

48. Putting it all Together on E and A

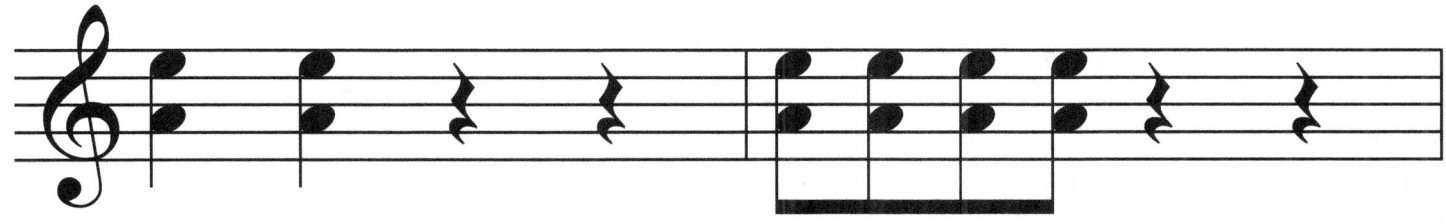

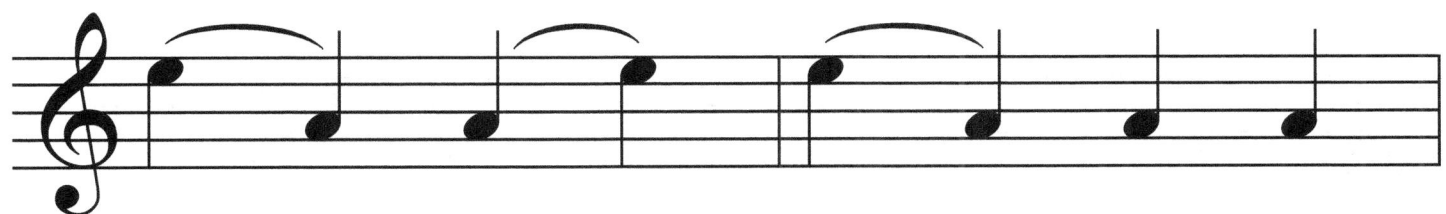

49. Putting it all Together on D and A

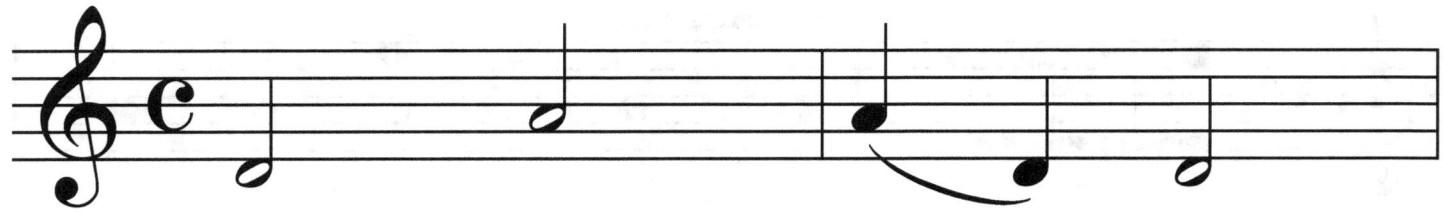

50. Putting it all Together on G and D

available from **www.charveypublications.com**: CHP317

First Position Scales for the Violin, Book One

G Major: First Octave

Cassia Harvey

©2017 C. Harvey Publications All Rights Reserved.

www.ingramcontent.com/pod-product-compliance
Lightning Source LLC
Chambersburg PA
CBHW051429070526
44584CB00023B/3647